[To the Galleries.

'Tis what you one and all approve?
For when you squeeze each other's hand,
And find your wishes at a stand,
You press the Wedding Day, and cry,
Come, let's to church, my dear, and try
Who loves the truest—you or I.
Then as 'tis known a day of bliss,
Pray let it not prove here amiss;
For tho' elop'd—I know not how—
From Next door Neighbours—just below—
And hither come to make her bow—
Like other trips of gallant love,
Constant to both you'll find her prove.
Or who is right, or who is wrong,
With me to state does not belong;
But only to proclaim the banns,
And leave to you th' applauding hands;
Nor hope to find one critic here
Will dare forbid our Wedding Cheer;
But give their usual friendly boon,
And let's enjoy the honey-moon.
To laugh is all our author means
In what she pourtrays in her scenes,
And aims, in all she dares to write,
To make her Wedding Day—a merry night.

ACT I

SCENE I

An Apartment at Lord Rakeland's

Enter a **SERVANT**, followed by **LORD RAKELAND**.

LORD RAKELAND
AT home? To be sure I am—how could you make any doubts about it?

[Exit **SERVANT**.

Deny me to my old acquaintance, and favourite friend, Tom Contest!

[Enter **MR CONTEST**.

My dear Contest, I congratulate us both that your travels are completed, and that you are come to taste, for the remainder of your life, the joys of your own country.

MR CONTEST
Whether to taste joy or sorrow I am yet in doubt; for I am uncertain in what manner I shall be received by my father.

LORD RAKELAND
Have not you seen him yet?

MR CONTEST
No:—nor dare I till I know in what humour he is.

LORD RAKELAND
In a good one, you may depend upon it; for he is very lately married.

MR CONTEST
To my utter concern! I heard some time ago indeed, that it was his design to marry again; but as he has never condescended to make me acquainted with it himself, I know nothing farther respecting the marriage than what public report has thrown in my way. Pray can you tell me who my new mother is?

LORD RAKELAND
I am told she is very young, extremely lively, and prodigiously beautiful. I am told too that she has been confined in the country, dressed, and treated like a child, till her present age of eighteen, in order to preserve the appearance of youth in her mother.

MR CONTEST
But who is her mother? Of what family is she?

LORD RAKELAND
That I don't know—and I suppose your father did not consider of what family she was, but merely what family she was likely to bring him.

MR CONTEST
Yes, I have no doubt but he married on purpose to disinherit me, for having written to him, "that I had fixed my affections upon a widow of small fortune, but one who was so perfectly to my wishes, that even his commands could not force me to forsake her."

LORD RAKELAND
And were you in earnest?

MR CONTEST
I thought I was then: but at present I am more humble. I have implored his pardon for those hasty expressions, and now only presume by supplication to obtain his approbation of my choice.

LORD RAKELAND
Is she a foreigner?

The Wedding Day by Mrs Inchbald

A COMEDY; IN TWO ACTS

AS PERFORMED AT THE THEATRE ROYAL, DRURY LANE

Elizabeth Simpson was born on 15th October 1753 at Stanningfield, near Bury St Edmunds, Suffolk.

Despite the fact that she suffered from a debilitating stammer she was determined to become an actress.

In April 1772, Elizabeth left, without permission, for London to pursue her chosen career. Although she was successful in obtaining parts her audiences, at first, found it difficult to admire her talents given her speech impediment. However, Elizabeth was diligent and hard-working on attempting to overcome this hurdle. She spent much time concentrating on pronunciation in order to eliminate the stammer. Her acting, although at times stilted, especially in monologues, gained praise for her approach for her well-developed characters.

That same year she married Joseph Inchbald and a few months later they appeared for the first time together on stage in 'King Lear'. The following month they toured Scotland with the West Digges's theatre company. This was to continue for several years.

Completely unexpectedly Joseph died in June 1779. It was now in the years after her husband's death that Elizabeth decided on a new literary path. With no attachments and acting taking up only some of her time she decided to write plays.

Her first play to be performed was 'A Mogul Tale or, The Descent of the Balloon', in 1784, in which she also played the leading female role of Selina. The play was premiered at the Haymarket Theatre.

One of the things that separated Elizabeth from other contemporary playwrights was her ability to translate plays from German and French into English for an audience that was ever-hungry for new works.

Her success as a playwright enabled Elizabeth to support herself and have no need of a husband to support her. Between 1784 and 1805 she had 19 of her comedies, sentimental dramas, and farces (many of them translations from the French) performed at London theatres. She is usually credited as Mrs Inchbald.

Mrs Elizabeth Inchbald died on 1st August 1821 in Kensington, London.

Index of Contents

PROLOGUE
ACT I
SCENE I - An Apartment at Lord Rakeland's
SCENE II - An Apartment at Sir Adam Contest's
ACT II
SCENE I - An Apartment at Mr. Millden's
SCENE II - An Apartment at Sir Adam Contests
MRS INCHBALD – A SHORT BIOGRAPHY
MRS INCHBALD – A CONCISE BIBLIOGRAPHY

DRAMATIS PERSONAE
MEN

Lord Rakeland	Mr. Barrymore
Sir Adam Contest	Mr. King
Mr. Millden	Mr. Packer
Mr. Contest	Mr. C. Kemble

WOMEN

Lady Autumn	Miss Tidswell
Lady Contest	Mrs. Jordan
Mrs. Hamford	Mrs. Hopkins
Hannah	Miss Heard
Several Servants.	

SCENE: London

TIME: One Day

THE WEDDING DAY: A COMEDY

PROLOGUE

BY **T. VAUGHAN, Esq**.

Spoken by **MR BARRYMORE**.

The title giv'n to our play
Is whimsical and odd, you'll say,
Because announc'd—The Wedding Day.
But know you not, my friends above,

MR CONTEST

No; an English woman.—We met at Florence—parted at Venice—and she arrived in London just four days before me.

LORD RAKELAND

And when will you introduce me to her?

MR CONTEST

Are you as much a man of gallantry as ever? If you are, you shall first promise me not to make love to her.

LORD RAKELAND

As to that, my dear friend, you know I never make a promise when I think there is the least probability of my breaking it.

MR CONTEST

Then positively you shall not see my choice till I am secure of her. But I can tell you what I'll do—I'll introduce you to my young mother-in-law, if you like.

LORD RAKELAND

My dear friend, that will do quite as well—nay, I don't know if it won't do better. Come, let us go directly.

MR CONTEST

Hold! not till I have obtained my father's leave:—for, after offending him so highly as not to hear from him these six months, I thought it necessary to send a letter to him as soon as I arrived this morning, to beg his permission to wait upon him. And here, I suppose, is his answer.

[Enter a **SERVANT**, and gives a letter to **MR CONTEST**.

SERVANT

Your servant enquired for you, Sir, and left this.

[Exit.

[**MR CONTEST** breaks open the letter hastily, and reads.

MR CONTEST

An invitation to go to his house immediately.
[He reads the remainder of the letter, and then expressing surprise]
—Why my father tells me he was only married this very morning! I heard he was married a week ago!

LORD RAKELAND

And so did I—and so did half the town. His marriage has even been in the newspapers these three days.

MR CONTEST

Ay, these things are always announced before they take place: and I most sincerely wish it had been delayed still longer.

LORD RAKELAND
I do not—for I long to have a kiss of the bride.

MR CONTEST
Pshaw! my Lord: as it is the wedding day, I cannot think of taking you now: it may be improper.

LORD RAKELAND
Not at all, not at all. A wedding day is a public day; and Sir Adam knows upon what familiar terms you and I are. Indeed, my dear friend, my going will be considered but as neighbourly. I can take no denial—I must go.

MR CONTEST
Well, if it must be so, come then.

[Going, stops.

Notwithstanding the cause I have for rejoicing at this kind invitation from my father, still I feel embarrassed at the thoughts of appearing before him, in the presence of his young wife; for I have no doubt but she'll take a dislike to me.

LORD RAKELAND
And if she should, I have no doubt but she'll take a liking to me. So come away, and be in spirits.

[Exeunt.

SCENE II

An Apartment at Sir Adam Contest's

Enter **SIR ADAM**, drest in white clothes like a Bridegroom.

SIR ADAM
Nothing is so provoking as to be in a situation where one is expected to be merry—it is like being asked in company "to tell a good story, and to be entertaining;" and then you are sure to be duller than ever you were in your life. Now, notwithstanding this is my wedding day, I am in such a blessed humour that I should like to make every person's life in this house a burthen to them. But I won't

[Struggling with himself

—No, I won't.—What a continual combat is mine! To feel a perpetual tendency to every vice, and to possess no one laudable quality, but that of a determination to overcome all my temptations. I am strongly impelled to violent anger, and yet I have the resolution to be a calm, peaceable man—I am inclined to suspicion, yet I conquer it, and will place confidence in others—I am disposed to malice, yet I constantly get the better of it—I am addicted to love, yet I—No, hold!—there I must stop—that is a failing which always did get the better of me. Behold an instance of it.

[Enter **LADY CONTEST** slowly and pensively, drest like a Bride.

SIR ADAM
Aside.
Now I will be in a good humour, in spite of all my doubts and fears.

LADY CONTEST
Did you send for me, Sir Adam?

SIR ADAM
Yes, my dear; your guardian is just stept home, to bring his wife to dine with us; and I wished to have a few minutes conversation with you. Sit down.

[They sit.

I observed, Lady Contest (and it gave me uneasiness), that at church this morning, while the ceremony was performing, you looked very pale. You have not yet wholly regained your colour: and instead of your usual cheerful countenance and air, I perceive a pensive, dejected—Come, look cheerful.
[Very sharply]
—Why don't you look cheerful?
[Checking himself, and softening his voice]
—Consider, every one should be happy upon their wedding day, for it is a day that seldom comes above once in a person's life.

LADY CONTEST
But with you, Sir Adam, it has come twice.

SIR ADAM
Very true—it has—and my first was a day indeed! I shall never forget it! My wife was as young as you are now—

LADY CONTEST
And you were younger than you are now.

SIR ADAM [Starts—then aside]
—No, I won't be angry.
[To her]
—She was beautiful too—nay more, she was good; she possessed every quality.—But this is not a proper topic on the present occasion; and so, my dear, let us change the subject.

LADY CONTEST
Pray, Sir Adam, is it true that your son is come to town?

SIR ADAM
It is; and I expect him here every moment.

LADY CONTEST

And have you invited no other company all day?

SIR ADAM
Your guardian and his wife, Mr. and Mrs. Ploughman, you know, will be here; and what other company would you have?

LADY CONTEST
In the country we had always fiddles and dancing at every wedding; and I declare I have been merrier at other people's weddings, than I think I am likely to be at my own.

SIR ADAM
If you loved me, Lady Contest, you would be merry in my company alone. Do you love me? My first wife loved me dearly.

LADY CONTEST
And so do I love you dearly—just the same as I would love my father, if he were alive.

SIR ADAM [Aside]
Now could I lay her at my feet for that sentence. But I won't—I won't.
[Struggling with himself]
Answer me this—would you change husbands with any one of your acquaintance?

LADY CONTEST
What signifies now my answering such a question as that, when I am sure not one of my acquaintance would change with me?

SIR ADAM [Violently]
What makes you think so?
[Softening]
—Your equipage will be by far the most splendid of any lady's you will visit. I have made good my promise in respect to your jewels too; and I hope you like them?

LADY CONTEST
Like them! to be sure!—Oh my dear Sir Adam, they even make me like you.

SIR ADAM
A very poor proof of your love, if you can give me no other.

LADY CONTEST
But I'll give you fifty others.

SIR ADAM [Anxiously]
Name them.

LADY CONTEST
First—I will always be obedient to you.

SIR ADAM

That's well.

LADY CONTEST
Second—I will never be angry with you if you should go out and stay for a month—nay, for a year—or for as long as ever you like.

SIR ADAM [Aside, and struggling with his passion]
Sure I was not born to commit murder? I had better go out of the room.

LADY CONTEST [Humming a tune]
"And old Robin Gray was kind to me."

SIR ADAM [Rising in agitation]
Oh my first wife, my first wife, what a treasure was she!
[Sighing]
But my treasure is gone!

LADY CONTEST
Not all your money, I hope, Sir Adam; for my guardian told me you had a great deal.

SIR ADAM
And did you marry me for that? What makes you blush? Come, confess to me—for there was always a sincerity in your nature which charmed me beyond your beauty. It was that sincerity, and that alone, which captivated me.

LADY CONTEST
Then I am surprised you did not marry your chaplain's widow, good old Mrs. Brown!

SIR ADAM
Why so?

LADY CONTEST
Because I have heard you say "there was not so sincere a woman on the face of the earth."

SIR ADAM [Aside]
And egad I almost wish I had married her. By what I have now said, Lady Contest, I meant to let you know, that in comparison with virtues, I have no esteem for a youthful or a beautiful face.

LADY CONTEST
Oh dear! how you and I differ! for I here declare, I do love a beautiful youthful face, better than I love any thing in the whole world.

SIR ADAM [In a half-smothered rage]
Leave the room—leave the room instantly.
[After a violent struggle]
No: Come back—come back, my dear—
[Tenderly. Aside]

I'll be in a good humour presently—but not just yet.—Yes—I will get the better of it.—I won't use her ill—I have sworn at the altar, not to use her ill, and I will keep my vow.
[He sits down affecting perfect composure, and after a pause]
—Pray, Lady Contest, pray, have not you heard from your mother yet?

LADY CONTEST
Not a line, nor a word.

SIR ADAM
It is wonderful that she should not send us a proper address! There is no doubt but that every letter we have sent to her since she has been abroad, has miscarried. However, it will be great joy and pride to her, when she hears of your marriage.

LADY CONTEST
Yes—for she always said I was not born to make my fortune.

SIR ADAM
Which prediction I have annulled. And after all—Come hither—come hither—

[Takes her kindly by the hand.

—And after all, I do not repent that I have—for although I cannot say that you possess all those qualifications which my first wife did, yet you behave very well considering your age.

LADY CONTEST
And I am sure so do you, considering yours.

SIR ADAM
All my resolution is gone, and I can keep my temper no longer.
[Aside]
Go into your own chamber immediately.

[He takes her by the hand and puts her off.

I'll—I'll—I'll—

[Threatening as if going to follow her, then stops short.

No, I'll go another way.

[As he is going off at the opposite side, enter a Servant].

SERVANT
My young master and another gentleman.

[Enter **MR CONTEST** and **LORD RAKELAND**

MR CONTEST To **SIR ADAM**]

I kneel, Sir, for your pardon and your blessing.

SIR ADAM
You have behaved very ill; but as you appear sensible of it, I forgive, and am glad to see you. But I expect that your future conduct shall give proof of your repentance. My Lord Rakeland, I beg pardon for introducing this subject before you; but you are not wholly unacquainted with it, I suppose?

LORD RAKELAND
Mr. Contest has partly informed me.
[Aside to **MR CONTEST**]
—Ask for your mother.

MR CONTEST
I sincerely congratulate you on your nuptials, Sir, and I hope Lady Contest is well.

SIR ADAM [Going to the side of the scene]
Desire Lady Contest to walk this way.

LORD RAKELAND
I, sincerely congratulate you, too, Sir Adam.

SIR ADAM
Thank you, my Lord, thank you.

[Enter **LADY CONTEST**. **SIR ADAM** takes her by the hand and presents **MR CONTEST** to her.

My dear, this is my son—and this, Tom, is your mother-in-law.

LADY CONTEST
Dear Sir Adam,
[Half laughing]
I was never so surprised in my life! Always when you spoke of your son you called him Tom, and Tommy, and I expected to see a little boy.

SIR ADAM
And have you any objection to his being a man?

LADY CONTEST
Oh no, I think I like him the better.
[To **MR CONTEST**]
—Sir, I am very glad to see you.

MR CONTEST
I give your Ladyship joy.

[Salutes her hand.

LADY CONTEST

I shall be very fond of him, Sir Adam—I shall like him as well as if he was my own.

SIR ADAM [Aside]
Now am I in a rage, lest seeing my son a man, she should be more powerfully reminded that I am old; and I long to turn him out of doors. But I won't—no—I'll be the kinder to him for this very suspicion. Come, Tom, let me shake hands with you—we have not shaken hands a great while; and let this be a sign of the full renewal of my paternal affection.

LORD RAKELAND
Sir Adam, you have not introduced me to Lady Contest.

LADY CONTEST
Is this another son?

SIR ADAM
What, could you be fond of him too?

LADY CONTEST
Yes, I could.

SIR ADAM
And like him as well as if he were your own?

LADY CONTEST
Yes, I could.

SIR ADAM
But he is not my son.

LADY CONTEST [Looking stedfastly at him]
I can't help thinking he is.

SIR ADAM
I tell you he is not.

LADY CONTEST
Nay, nay, you are joking—I am sure he is.

SIR ADAM [Raising his voice]
I tell you, no.

LADY CONTEST
Why he is very like you.

[She goes up to **LORD RAKELAND**, and looks in his face.

No, he is not so like when you are close. I beg ten thousand pardons, Sir, you are not at all like Sir Adam.

SIR ADAM [Aside]

Zounds, now I am jealous—and I am afraid my propensity will get the better of me. But no, it shan't—No, it shall not.—My Lord, I beg your pardon, but I want half an hour's private conversation with my son; will you excuse us?

LORD RAKELAND

Certainly, Sir Adam—I beg you will make no stranger of me.

SIR ADAM [Taking **MR CONTEST** by the hand]

Come, Tom.

[Aside]

—There, now, I have left them alone; and I think this is triumphing over my jealousy pretty well. Well done, Sir Adam, well done, well done.

[Exit with **MR CONTEST**, **SIR ADAM** smiling with self-applause at the victory he has gained.

LORD RAKELAND

My dear Lady Contest, though I acknowledge I have not the happiness to be your son, yet, permit me to beg a blessing on my knees—'Tis this—Tell me when and where I shall have the happiness of seeing you again?

LADY CONTEST

Dear Sir, without any compliment, the happiness will be done to me.

LORD RAKELAND

Enchanting woman! appoint the time.

LADY CONTEST

I'll ask Sir Adam.

LORD RAKELAND

No—without his being present.

LADY CONTEST

I don't know if I sha'n't like that full as well.

LORD RAKELAND

Appoint a time, then; just to play a game at cribbage.

LADY CONTEST

Or what do you think of "Beggar my Neighbour?"—would not that do as well?

LORD RAKELAND

Perfectly as well. The very thing.

LADY CONTEST

But you must take care how you play; for it is a game you may lose a great deal of money by.

LORD RAKELAND
But Sir Adam must not know of it.

[Enter **SIR ADAM**, and speaks aside.

SIR ADAM
Resolutions come and go—I wish I could have kept mine, and staid away a little longer.
[Affecting good humour]
What, my Lord, here still? holding conversation with this giddy woman?

LORD RAKELAND [Affecting coldness]
I assure you, Sir Adam, I am very well pleased with Lady Contest's conversation.

LADY CONTEST
And I am sure, my Lord, I am very much pleased with yours.

LORD RAKELAND
We have been talking about a game at cards.

LADY CONTEST
But you said Sir Adam was not to be of the party.

LORD RAKELAND
Yes, Sir Adam—but not Mr. Contest.

LADY CONTEST
No, indeed you said Sir Adam.

LORD RAKELAND
Oh no.

LADY CONTEST [Eagerly]
Yes—because, don't you remember I said—and you made answer—

LORD RAKELAND
I don't remember any thing—

LADY CONTEST
What! don't you remember kneeling for my blessing?

SIR ADAM
How! What!

LORD RAKELAND
Sir Adam, it would be a breach of good manners were I to contradict Lady Contest a second time; therefore I acknowledge that she is right—and that I have been in the wrong.

[Exit, bowing with great respect.

LADY CONTEST [To **SIR ADAM** apart, and pulling his sleeve]
Won't you ask him to dinner?

SIR ADAM
Ask him to dinner! What a difference between you and my first wife!—Would she have wished me to ask him to dinner? would she have suffered a man to kneel—

LADY CONTEST
I did not suffer him to kneel a moment.

SIR ADAM
—But my first wife was a model of perfection, and it is unjust to reproach you with the comparison. Yet I cannot help saying—would she had lived!

LADY CONTEST
And I am sure I wish so, with all my heart.

SIR ADAM [Fetching a heavy sigh]
But she was suddenly snatched from me.

LADY CONTEST
How was it, Sir Adam? Were you not at sea together? And so a storm arose—and so you took to the long-boat—and she would stay in the ship—and so she called to you, and you would not go—and you called to her, and she would not come. And so your boat sailed, and her ship sunk.

SIR ADAM
Don't, don't—I can't bear to hear it repeated. I loved her too sincerely. But the only proof I can now give of my affection, is to be kind to her son; and as by what he acknowledged to me, his heart I perceived was bent upon marriage, I have given him leave to introduce to me the lady on whom he has fixed his choice—and if I like her—

LADY CONTEST
Has he fixed his choice? Who is the young lady? What is her name?

SIR ADAM
I did not ask her name.

LADY CONTEST
But I hope you will give your consent, whoever she is.

SIR ADAM
And if I do, in a little time they may both wish I had not. Young people are so capricious they don't know their own minds half an hour. For instance, I dare say you think very highly of that young Lord who was here just now; but if you were to see him two or three times a week, you would cease to admire him.

LADY CONTEST
I should like to try. Do invite him here two or three times a week, on purpose to try.

[Enter **SERVANT**.

SERVANT
Mr. and Mrs. Ploughman are come, Sir, and dinner is almost ready.

[Exit.

LADY CONTEST [Looking at her hand, gives a violent scream]
Oh! Oh!—Oh dear! Sir Adam—Oh dear! Oh dear! Oh dear!

SIR ADAM
What's the matter? What in the name of heaven is the matter?

LADY CONTEST
I wish I may die if I have not lost my wedding ring.—Oh! 'tis a sure sign of some ill luck.

SIR ADAM
Here, John!

[Enter **SERVANT**.

Go and look for your mistress's wedding ring; she has dropt it somewhere about the house.

LADY CONTEST
I am afraid it was in the street, as I stepp'd out of my coach. Oh! indeed, Sir Adam, it did not stick close. I remember I pulled my glove off just at that time; go and look there, John.

[Exit **SERVANT**.

Oh! Sir Adam, some ill luck will certainly happen to one or both of us: you may depend upon it.

SIR ADAM
Childish nonsense! What ill luck can happen to us while we are good?

LADY CONTEST
But suppose we should not be good?

SIR ADAM
We always may if we please.

LADY CONTEST
I know we may. But then sometimes 'tis a great deal of trouble.

SIR ADAM
Come, don't frighten yourself about omens; you'll find your ring again.

LADY CONTEST

Do you think that young Lord mayn't have found it? Suppose we send to ask him?

SIR ADAM
Did you miss it while he was here?

LADY CONTEST
No, nor should not have missed any thing, if he had staid till midnight.

SIR ADAM [Taking her by the hand]
Come, come to dinner.

[Going, stops.

But I must say this has been a very careless thing of you. My first wife would not have lost her wedding ring.

LADY CONTEST
But indeed, Sir Adam, mine did not fit.

[Exeunt.

ACT II

SCENE I

An Apartment at Mr. Millden's

[Enter **LADY AUTUMN** and **MRS HAMFORD**.

MRS HAMFORD.
MY dear Lady Autumn, Mr. Contest is not of a proper age for a lover, much less for a husband of yours.

LADY AUTUMN
Mrs. Hamford, I believe, old as you pretend to think me now, you thought me young but a few weeks ago at Venice; when, on your first landing there, you imposed upon me your romantic tale, and prevailed with me to bring you to England.

MRS HAMFORD
Hold, Madam, do not conclude too hastily, that, because I have for a few days since my arrival in my native country, deferred my promise of revealing to you my real name and my connections here, that I am for this reason an impostor.

LADY AUTUMN
No; upon recollection, you certainly have been living on a savage island for these ten or twelve years, which gives you all these Hottentot ideas in respect to the advanced age of women. In some savage countries women are old at seventeen; but in this enlightened nation we are all young at seventy.

[Enter **MR MILLDEN**.

MR MILLDEN
Lady Autumn, I make no apology for entering your apartment thus abruptly, because I come with good news—Your daughter is married.

LADY AUTUMN
Married! What! while I have been abroad?

MR MILLDEN
No doubt—But I cannot give you any particulars of the marriage, nor tell you even the gentleman's name—for I only passed her guardian by accident in his carriage, and I had not an opportunity to enquire, nor he to inform me farther, than "that it was a most advantageous union for your daughter, for that her husband is a man of fortune and title."

MRS HAMFORD
There, Lady Autumn! you find you have a daughter old enough to be a wife.

LADY AUTUMN
More shame for her—Why was not my consent asked?

MR MILLDEN
You were out of England, and no letters reached you. However, your daughter's guardian will call upon you in the evening, and explain to you every particular.

LADY AUTUMN
But now, my dear Mr. Millden, and you my dear Mrs. Hamford, don't let this marriage escape your lips, if Mr. Contest should call this evening—for if my daughter's husband should not, after all, be a man of some importance, I should wish to keep it a secret from Mr. Contest that I have a daughter married.

[Exit.

MR MILLDEN
Mrs. Hamford, I observe a gloom upon your countenance; I hope no enquiries you have made concerning any part of your family since you arrived in England—
[He takes her hand]
—You tremble! What's the matter?

MRS HAMFORD
I tremble till a visit which I am now going to make is over; and then, whatever is my destiny, I trust in that Power which has supported me through numerous trials, to give me resignation.

[Exeunt.

SCENE II

Enter **LADY CONTEST**, followed by her **MAID**.

LADY CONTEST [Pulling off her cloak]
Has any body called on me, Hannah, since I have been out?

HANNAH
Yes, Madam, an elderly gentlewoman; but she refused to leave her name—she said she had particular business, and wanted to speak to you in private.

LADY CONTEST
Then pray let me see her when she comes again.

HANNAH
I told her, Madam, that you were only gone to the milliner's in the next street.

LADY CONTEST
Has any body else called, Hannah?

HANNAH
No, ma'am.

[Enter a **SERVANT**.

SERVANT
Lord Rakeland, if your Ladyship is not engaged—

LADY CONTEST [Drawing **HANNAH** on one side]
Oh! Hannah, Hannah! is this the elderly gentlewoman?—Oh! for shame, Hannah!—However, poor Hannah, don't be uneasy. I won't be very angry with you.
[To the **SERVANT**]
You may desire his Lordship to walk up.

[Exit **SERVANT**.

HANNAH
Upon my word, my lady—

LADY CONTEST
Oh, hold your tongue, Hannah—you know this is the elderly gentlewoman you meant—but no matter—I am almost every bit as well pleased.

[Enter **LORD RAKELAND**

[Exit **HANNAH**.

LORD RAKELAND
My adorable Lady Contest—

LADY CONTEST
I hope you are very well—but I need not ask, for you look charmingly.

LORD RAKELAND
And you look like a divinity! I met Sir Adam this moment in his carriage going out, and that emboldened me—

LADY CONTEST
Yes, Sir, he is gone out for a little while with my guardian; but he'll soon be back. I suppose, Sir, you called to play an hand of cards.

LORD RAKELAND
No—my errand was to tell you—I love you; I adore you; and to plead for your love in return.

LADY CONTEST
But that is not in my power to give.

LORD RAKELAND
You cannot possibly have given it to Sir Adam!

LADY CONTEST
I sha'n't tell you what I have done with it.

LORD RAKELAND
You could love me; I know you could.

LADY CONTEST
If you were my husband I would try: and then, perhaps, take all the pains I would, I could not.

LORD RAKELAND
Oh! that I were your husband!

[Kneeling.

LADY CONTEST
You would not kneel so if you were. Not even on the wedding day.

LORD RAKELAND [Throwing his arms about her.
No, but I would clasp you thus.

LADY CONTEST
Oh dear! Oh dear! I am afraid Sir Adam's first wife would not have suffered this!

LORD RAKELAND
Why talk of Sir Adam? Oh! that you were mine, instead of his!

LADY CONTEST
And would you really marry me, if I were single?

LORD RAKELAND
Would I?—yes—this instant, were you unmarried, this instant, with rapture, I would become your happy bridegroom.

LADY CONTEST
I wonder what Sir Adam would say were he to hear you talk thus! He suspected you were in love with me at the very first—I can't say I did—I suspected nothing—but I have found a great deal.

LORD RAKELAND
Nothing to my disadvantage, I hope?

LADY CONTEST
No—nor any thing that shall be of disadvantage to Sir Adam.

LORD RAKELAND
Why are you perpetually talking of your husband?

LADY CONTEST
Because, when I am in your company, I am always thinking of him.

LORD RAKELAND
Do I make you think of your husband?

LADY CONTEST
Yes—and you make me tremble for him.

LORD RAKELAND
Never be unhappy about Sir Adam.

LADY CONTEST
I won't—and he shall never have cause to be unhappy about me—for I'll go lock myself up till he comes home.

[Going.

LORD RAKELAND [Holding her]
What are you alarmed at? Is there any thing to terrify you either in my countenance or address?—In your presence, I feel myself an object of pity, not of terror.

LADY CONTEST
Ay, but this may be all make-believe, like the poor little boy in the song.

SONG.
I.

In the dead of the night, when, with labour opprest,
All mortals enjoy the calm blessing of ease,
Cupid knock'd at my window, disturbing my rest,
Who's there? I demanded—Begone, if you please.

II.
He answer'd so meekly, so modest, and mild,
Dear ma'am, it is I, an unfortunate child;
'Tis a cold rainy night, I am wet to the skin;
I have lost my way, ma'am, so pray let me in.

III.
No sooner from wet and from cold he got ease,
Then taking his bow he cry'd, Ma'am, if you please,
If you please, ma'am, I would by experiment know
If the rain has damaged the string of my bow.

IV.
Then away skipp'd the urchin, as brisk as a bee,
And, laughing, I wish you much joy, ma'am, said he;
My bow is undamag'd, for true went the dart,
But you will have trouble enough with your heart.

[Going.

[Enter **SERVANT**.

SERVANT
A lady, a stranger, who Mrs Hannah says your Ladyship gave orders should be admitted—

LADY CONTEST
Very true—Desire her to walk in—shew her up.

[Exit **SERVANT**.

LORD RAKELAND
Who is it?

LADY CONTEST
I don't know—I can't tell—I thought you had been her: but I was mistaken.

LORD RAKELAND
Will she stay long?

LADY CONTEST
I don't know any thing about her.

LORD RAKELAND

Dear Lady Contest, do not let me meet her on the stairs; conceal me somewhere till she is gone. Here, I'll go into this dressing-room.

[He goes to a door, which leads to the next chamber.

LADY CONTEST
Then you will hear our discourse.

LORD RAKELAND
No matter; I will keep it a secret.

LADY CONTEST
No, no; you must go away—out of the house.

LORD RAKELAND
I can't—I won't—don't expose yourself before the lady.

[Enter **MRS HAMFORD**

[**LORD RAKELAND** goes into the next room; but stands at the door, and listens to the conversation of the ensuing scene.

MRS HAMFORD [Curtseying to **LADY CONTEST**]
—I beg pardon, Madam.

LADY CONTEST [Curtseying]
—No apologies, Madam.

MRS HAMFORD
I am afraid I am not right!

[Looking round.

LADY CONTEST
Yes, Madam—Pray are not you the lady who called this afternoon, and said you had particular business?

MRS HAMFORD
I am.
[Looking earnestly at her]
—And are you Lady Contest?

LADY CONTEST
Yes, Ma'am.

MRS HAMFORD [In surprise]
Sir Adam's wife?

LADY CONTEST

Yes, Ma'am, Sir Adam's wife—Won't you please to sit down?

[They sit.

MRS HAMFORD
There is then, Lady Contest, a very material circumstance in my life, that I wish to reveal to you; and to receive from you advice how to act, rather than by confiding in the judgment of any of my own family, be flattered, by their partiality, into a blameable system of conduct. Such is the nature of my present errand to you: but, to my great surprise, I find you so very, very young—

LADY CONTEST
Yes, Ma'am, thank heaven.

MRS HAMFORD
And you are very happy, I presume?

LADY CONTEST [Hesitating]
—Y-e-s, Ma'am—yes, very happy, all things considered.

MRS HAMFORD
I am sorry then to be the messenger of news that will, most probably, destroy that happiness for ever.

LADY CONTEST [Rising]
Dear me! what news? You frighten me out of my wits!

MRS HAMFORD
You are now, Lady Contest, newly married; in the height of youth, health, prosperity; and I am the fatal object who, in one moment, may crush all those joys!

LADY CONTEST
Oh! then pray don't—you'll break my heart if you do. What have I done, or what has happened to take away from me all my joys?—Where's my pocket handkerchief?

[Feeling in her pocket.

MRS HAMFORD
Here, take mine, and compose yourself.

LADY CONTEST [Taking it]
—Thank you, Ma'am.

MRS HAMFORD
And now, my dear, I will inform you—and at the same time flatter myself that you will deal frankly with me, and not restrain any of those sensations which my tale may cause.

LADY CONTEST
Dear Madam, I never conceal any of my sensations—I can't if I would.

MRS HAMFORD
Then what will they be when I tell you—I am Sir Adam Contest's wife—his wife whom he thinks drowned; but who was preserved and restored to life, though not till now restored to my own country.

LADY CONTEST
Dear Madam, I don't know any body on earth I should be happier to see!

[Runs to her, embraces, and hugs her repeatedly.

MRS HAMFORD
But consider, my dear, you are no longer wife to Sir Adam!

LADY CONTEST
And is that all?—here, take your handkerchief again.
[Returns it her]
And come you out of your hiding place.

[She goes to the chamber where **LORD RAKELAND** is—He enters confused, and bowing to **MRS HAMFORD**.

—Come, come, for you need no longer conceal yourself now, or be miserable; for I have no longer a husband to prevent my being your wife—or to prevent me from loving you—for oh! oh! I do—
[Checks herself]
—though I durst not say so before.

MRS HAMFORD
May I enquire who this gentleman is?

LADY CONTEST
A poor man that has been dying for love of me, even though he thought it a sin.

LORD RAKELAND
I beg pardon, and promise never to be guilty for the future.—I wish you a good evening.

[Going.

LADY CONTEST
You are not going away?

LORD RAKELAND
I have an engagement it is impossible to postpone.—Good evening.

LADY CONTEST
But you will soon come back, I hope?—for I suppose you hold your mind to be my husband?

LORD RAKELAND
Alas! that is a happiness above my hopes.

LADY CONTEST
Above your hopes!

LORD RAKELAND
It is.

LADY CONTEST
Then it shall be beneath mine.

[He bows, and exit.

MRS HAMFORD
And is it possible that you can think of parting with Sir Adam without the least reluctance?

LADY CONTEST
Pray, Madam, when did you see Sir Adam last?

MRS HAMFORD
Above fifteen years ago.

LADY CONTEST
He is greatly altered since that time.

MRS HAMFORD
Still will my affection be the same.

LADY CONTEST
And so it ought; for he loves you still—he is for ever talking of you; and declares he never knew what happiness was since he lost you. Oh! he will be so pleased to change me for you!

MRS HAMFORD
I hope you do not flatter me!

LADY CONTEST
I am sure I don't—I expect him at home every minute, and then you'll see!

MRS HAMFORD
Excuse me—At present I could not support an interview. I will take my leave till I hear from you; and will confide in your artless and ingenuous friendship to inform Sir Adam of my escape.

LADY CONTEST
You may depend upon me, Lady Contest.

MRS HAMFORD
Adieu!

[Going.

LADY CONTEST
Dear Madam, I would insist on waiting upon you down stairs; but I won't stand upon any ceremony with you in your own house.

[Exit **MRS HAMFORD**

[As **LADY CONTEST** is going off at the opposite side, she stops on hearing **SIR ADAM'S** voice without.

SIR ADAM
Nobody so plagued as I am with servants!

[Enter **SIR ADAM.**

LADY CONTEST
Bless me, Sir Adam, I did not know you were come home!

SIR ADAM
I have been at home this quarter of an hour. The coachman has made himself tipsy on the joyful occasion of our marriage, and was very near dashing out my brains in turning a corner.

LADY CONTEST
And is that worth being in such an ill temper about?—Ah! you would not be so cross, if you knew something.

SIR ADAM
Knew what?—I have a piece of news to tell you.

LADY CONTEST
And I have a piece of news to tell you.

SIR ADAM
Your mother is arrived in town: your guardian heard so this morning, but he did not mention it to me till this moment, because he thinks it is proper for him to wait upon, and acquaint her with our marriage in form, before I throw myself at her feet, to ask her blessing.

LADY CONTEST
Very well—with all my heart. And now, Sir Adam—what do you think?

SIR ADAM
What do I think!

LADY CONTEST
What will you give me to tell you something that will make you go almost out of your wits with joy?

SIR ADAM
What do you mean?—Have I got another estate left me?

LADY CONTEST

No: something better.

SIR ADAM
Better than that!

LADY CONTEST
A great deal better—you will think.

SIR ADAM [Eagerly]
—Has the county meeting agreed to elect me their representative?

LADY CONTEST
No.

SIR ADAM
What any thing better than that?

LADY CONTEST
A great deal better than that—and something the most surprising!—Guess again.

SIR ADAM
Pshaw! I'll guess no more—I hate such teazing—it is unmannerly—would my first wife have served me so?

LADY CONTEST
Now you have hit upon it.

SIR ADAM
Upon what?

LADY CONTEST
Your first wife.

SIR ADAM
Ay, I shall never see her like again!

LADY CONTEST
No, but you may see her—for she is alive, and you may have her home as soon as you please.

SIR ADAM [Trembling]
What the deuce does the woman mean?

LADY CONTEST
Your first wife—escaped in the long boat—as surprising a story as Robinson Crusoe!—I have seen her, and she longs to see you.

SIR ADAM
Why, what do you mean?—

[Still trembling]
Alive?

LADY CONTEST
As much alive as I am.

SIR ADAM
And what does she intend to do?—
[Trembling]
Poor woman! poor creature! where does she intend to go?

LADY CONTEST
Go! Come home, to be sure.

SIR ADAM
Home!—what does she call her home?

LADY CONTEST
You are her home.

SIR ADAM
I her home!—Come to me!—What can I do with her?—and what is to become of you?

LADY CONTEST
Oh! never mind me.

SIR ADAM
Yes, but I can't think to part with you—
[Ready to cry]
I can't think to turn a poor young creature like you upon the wide world.—Her age will secure her; she won't be in half the danger.

LADY CONTEST
Poor soul! if you knew what she has suffered—

SIR ADAM
And have not I suffered too? I am sure I have lamented her loss every hour of my life; you have heard me.

LADY CONTEST
And yet you don't seem half so much pleased at her return as I am.

SIR ADAM
I cannot help being concerned to think, what a melancholy twelve or fourteen years the poor woman has experienced! most likely upon some desert island, instead of being in heaven!

LADY CONTEST
But if you are concerned upon her account, you ought to be pleased upon your own, my dear—

[Checks herself]
I beg pardon; I mean Sir Adam.

SIR ADAM
No, no, call me "my dear"—do not shew reserve to me already; for if you do, you will break my heart.

LADY CONTEST
I would not break your heart for the world—and indeed, Sir Adam—you will always be dear to me—quite as dear when we are parted, nay, I think, dearer than if we were living together.

SIR ADAM
Don't talk of parting—Can you resolve to part from me?

LADY CONTEST
Yes, because I know you will be so much happier with your first wife.

SIR ADAM
But if our parting should give you any uneasiness—

LADY CONTEST
It won't a bit.

SIR ADAM
No!

LADY CONTEST
No,
[Soothing]
—not when I know you are with that good, prudent woman, your first wife.

SIR ADAM [Aside]
—Now here is a time to exert my power over myself: what signifies having exerted it in trivial matters, if from a trial such as this I shrink?—
[To her]
—making many efforts to get rid of his feelings
—Well, Madam, I am prepared to see my first wife—and to part with my second.

LADY CONTEST
Then sit down and write to her, that you long to see her.

SIR ADAM
No! I can sacrifice all my sensations, but I cannot sacrifice truth.

LADY CONTEST
Will you give me leave to write to her, a kind letter for you, and invite her to come hither directly?

SIR ADAM [After a struggle]
—You may do as you like.

LADY CONTEST
Ay, I shan't be with you long, and so you may as well let me have my own way while I stay.—

[She writes—he walks about, starts, and shews various signs of uneasiness during the time.

LADY CONTEST
Here they are; only a few words, but very kind; telling her to "fly to your impatient wishes." Here, John—

[Enter **SERVANT**.

—Take this letter to Mr. Millden's immediately.

[Exit **SERVANT**.

[She goes to **SIR ADAM**.

—Come, look pleased; consider how charming it is for old friends to meet.

SIR ADAM
Yes, if they are not too old. However, fear nothing in regard to my conduct, for I will, I will act properly—so properly, that I will not trust my own judgment; and the first person I consult shall be your mother, and I'll go to her this instant.
[Going]
—Sure never such a strange, intricate affair ever happened before!—but strange as it is, I will act as I ought to do—My inclination may rebel, but my reason shall conquer—I will act as I ought to do.

[Enter **SERVANT**.

SERVANT
Lady Autumn and Mr. Contest.

SIR ADAM
And here your mother comes most opportunely.

[Enter **MR CONTEST** and **LADY AUTUMN**

MR CONTEST
Sir Adam, according to your permission, I have brought the lady on whom I have placed my affections, to receive from—

LADY CONTEST
Oh my dear mother, how do you do?

[Running to **LADY AUTUMN**.

MR CONTEST
Mother!—Your mother!

LADY CONTEST
Yes—though she looks very well, does not she?

MR CONTEST
This is the lady on whom I have fixed my choice.

LADY CONTEST
What, on my mamma! Nay, Mr. Contest, now I am sure you are joking—ha, ha, ha, ha,—ha, ha, ha, ha,—fixed your choice on my mother!

SIR ADAM
And my mother! your father's mother!—Why you are as bad as the man in the farce—fall in love with your grandmother.

LADY CONTEST
Dear mamma, don't make yourself uneasy, if you have a mind to marry my son; for there is a lady now at Mr. Millden's, and who is coming here, that will claim him for her son, and make me no longer wife to Sir Adam.

LADY AUTUMN
This can be no other than Mrs. Hamford, whom I brought to England.

[Enter **MR MILLDEN**

MR MILLDEN
Mr. Contest, will you step for a moment to the person in the next room.

[Exit **MR CONTEST**.

Sir Adam Contest, I come to inform you, that there is a lady in the next room who has been near fainting at the sound of your voice.

SIR ADAM
And I believe I shall faint at the sound of her's.

MR MILLDEN
Her son is supporting her to you.

[Enter **MRS HAMFORD** leaning on **MR CONTEST.**

LADY CONTEST
Dear Sir Adam, fly and embrace your first wife.
[She goes to her]
—Dear Lady Contest, notwithstanding his seeming insensibility he loves you to distraction: a thousand times has he declared to me, he did not think there was such a woman in the world.

SIR ADAM

And I did flatter myself, there was not.

MRS HAMFORD [Seeing **SIR ADAM** advance towards her]
—Oh! Sir Adam!

SIR ADAM
Oh my dear! If you knew what I have suffered, and what I still suffer on your account, you would pity me.

LADY AUTUMN
Sir Adam, I give you joy of a wife that suits your own age.

SIR ADAM
And such a one shall my son marry, when he has my consent.

MRS HAMFORD
Come, come, Sir Adam and Lady Autumn, these mutual reproaches, for almost the self-same fault, ought to convince you, that in your plans of wedlock you have both been wrong.

SIR ADAM
However, it shall be my endeavour to be henceforward right: for after settling upon my young bride a handsome dower, I will peaceably yield her up;—and though it is a hard struggle, yet, like all my other struggles, it will, I have no doubt, give me happiness in the end.

LADY CONTEST [Crying till she sobs]
Good b'ye, Sir Adam—good b'ye—I did love you a little upon my word; and if I was not sure you were going to be so much happier with your first wife, I should never know a moment's peace.
SIR ADAM
I thank you. And at parting, all I have to request of you is—that you will not marry again till I die.

LADY CONTEST
Indeed, Sir Adam, I will not—but then you won't make it long?

SIR ADAM
I believe I shan't.

LADY CONTEST
And my next husband shall be of my own age; but he shall possess, Sir Adam, your principles of honour. And then, if my wedding ring should unhappily sit loose, I will guard it with unwearied discretion: and I will hold it sacred—even though it should pinch my finger.

Mrs Inchbald – A Short Biography

Elizabeth Simpson was born on 15th October 1753 at Stanningfield, near Bury St Edmunds, Suffolk. She was the eighth of nine children to John Simpson, a farmer, and his wife, Mary, née Rushbrook. The family were Roman Catholics.

Her brother was educated at school, but Elizabeth, like her sisters, was educated at home. Elizabeth also suffered from a speech impediment, a stammer.

Elizabeth's father had died when she was only eight, leaving her mother to take care of a large family. These were difficult times.

Despite the fact that she suffered from a debilitating stammer she was determined, from a very young age, to become an actress. She had loved theatre from her very first childhood visit.

As a young woman Elizabeth was tall and slender. But this beauty brought with it the many attentions of men. It was double-edged.

Elizabeth had written to the manager of the Norwich Theatre to obtain acting work. He had replied that he would welcome a visit for her to audition. For her young naïve years this seemed like a golden opportunity. However, in 1770 her family forbade her attempt to take on an acting assignment there. They had no such qualms with her brother George, who entered the acting profession.

In April 1772, Elizabeth left, without permission, for London to pursue her chosen career. Although she was successful in obtaining parts her audiences found it difficult to admire her talents given her speech impediment. However, Elizabeth was diligent and hard-working on attempting to overcome this hurdle. She spent much time concentrating on pronunciation in order to eliminate the stammer. She was known to write out the parts she wanted to perform and practice the lines to point of such familiarity that her impediment was banished. Her acting, although at times stilted, especially in monologues, gained praise for her approach, and for her well-developed characters. For the audience she came across as a real person, not just an actor performing a piece. Elizabeth would keenly study the performances of others before she herself performed.

In these early months Elizabeth was young and alone, and reportedly also suffered from the attentions of sexual predators.

In June, merely two months after arriving she accepted an offer of marriage from Joseph Inchbald, a fellow Catholic and actor. They had met before on her previous trips to London, usually to see her brother, George, acting on stage. He had written her several letters proposing marriage which she had declined. But now it seemed the most expedient way to make progress in her career.

By all accounts it was still an odd choice. Joseph was a so-so actor, and at least twice her age as well as being the father of two illegitimate sons. The marriage was to produce no children and was not the happiest of unions.

On 4th September of that year, 1772, Elizabeth and Joseph appeared for the first time together on stage in 'King Lear'. The following month they toured Scotland with the West Digges's theatre company. This was to continue for the next four years.

In 1776 they decided on a change of career and a change of country. They moved to France. Joseph would now learn to paint, and Elizabeth would study French. It was a short-lived disaster. Within a month all their funds were gone and a return to England was necessitated.

They moved to Liverpool, Canterbury and Yorkshire and acted for both the Joseph Younger's company and Tate Wilkinson's company in search of permanency and a recovery from their ill-fortune.

Completely unexpectedly Joseph died in June 1779. Despite her loss Elizabeth continued to perform across the country from Dublin to London and places in between.

In 1780, she joined the Covent Garden Company and played Bellarion in 'Philaster'.

In all Elizabeth's acting career was only moderately successful and lasted some 17 years. However, she appeared in many classical roles as well as new plays such as Hannah Cowley's 'The Belle's Stratagem'. Around the theatre she was known for upholding high moral standards. She later described having to fend off sexual advances from, among others, stage manager James Dodd and theatre manager John Taylor.

It was now in the years after her husband's death that that Elizabeth decided on a new literary path. With no attachments, and acting taking up only some of her time, she decided to write plays.

Her first play to be performed was 'A Mogul Tale or, The Descent of the Balloon', in 1784, in which she also played the leading female role of Selina. The play was premiered at the Haymarket Theatre.

'Lovers' Vows', in 1798, was based on her translation of August von Kotzebues original work and garnered both praise and complements from Jane Austen and was featured as a focus of moral controversy in her novel Mansfield Park. Although Austen's book brought more fame to Elizabeth, 'Lovers' Vows' initially ran for only forty-two nights when originally performed in 1798.

One of the things that separated Elizabeth from other contemporary playwrights was her ability to translate plays from German and French into English and to use them as a foundation. These translations were popular with the public and her talents in bringing the characters to life was instrumental in achieving this.

Her success as a playwright enabled Elizabeth to support herself and not need a new husband to carry out this role. Between 1784 and 1805 she had 19 of her comedies, sentimental dramas, and farces (many of them translations from the French) performed at London theatres, although it is thought she actually wrote between 21 and 23 in total depending on which account you think is most accurate. She is usually credited as Mrs Inchbald.

As well she wrote two novels; 'A Simple Story' was published in 1791 and once referred to as "the most elegant English fiction of the eighteenth century". 'Nature and Art' was published in 1796. Both have been constantly reprinted.

Her four-volume autobiography was destroyed before her death upon the advice of her confessor, but she left a few of her diaries.

In her later years she found time to do a considerable amount of editorial and critical work. In 1805, she decided to try being a theatre critic. This literary excursion, after the praise for her acting and more so for her writing, seemed to be a low point in her achievements. The reception to her work amongst her peer critics was low, one commented upon her ignorance of Shakespeare.

Her career from actress, to playwright and novelist was achieved in difficult times for women to accomplish such things. Indeed, whilst the theatre and its boundaries were quite strict she managed, in her novels, to explore political radicalism. Her good looks together with her passionate and fiery nature attracted a string of admirers but she never re-married. Despite her love of independence, she still desired and sought social respectability.

Mrs Elizabeth Inchbald died on 1st August 1821 in Kensington, London.

She is buried in the churchyard of St Mary Abbots. On her gravestone is written, "Whose writings will be cherished while truth, simplicity, and feelings, command public admiration."

Mrs Inchbald – A Concise Bibliography

Plays
Mogul Tale; or, The Descent of the Balloon (1784)
Appearance is against Them (1785)
I'll Tell you What (1785)
The Widow's Vow (1786)
The Midnight Hour (1787)
Such Things Are (1787)
All on a Summer's Day (1787)
Animal Magnetism (c1788)
The Child of Nature (1788)
The Married Man (1789)
Next Door Neighbours (1791)
Everyone has his Fault (1793)
To Marry, or not to Marry (1793)
The Wedding Day (1794)
Wives as They Were and Maids as They Are (1797)
Lovers' Vows (1798)
The Wise Man of the East (1799)
The Massacre (1792 (not performed)
A Case of Conscience (published 1833)
The Ancient Law (not performed)
The Hue and Cry (unpublished)
Young Men and Old Women (Lovers No Conjurers) (adaptation of Le Méchant; unpublished)

Novels

A Simple Story (1791)
Nature and Art (1796)